Learn Poker

in 10 minutes

Brian Byfield

Illustrations by Gray Jolliffe

BATSFORD

First published in the United Kingdom in 2013 by
Batsford, 10 Southcombe Street, London W14 0RA

An imprint of Anova Books Company Ltd

ISBN 978 1 84994 060 3

A CIP catalogue record for this book is available
from the British Library.

20 19 18 17 16 15 14 13
10 9 8 7 6 5 4 3 2 1

Reproduction by Rival Colour Ltd, UK
Printed and bound by 1010 Printing International Ltd, China

Introduction

If you want to play cards for money, poker is the
ultimate gambling game. Learning to play is the
easy part, but walking away with the money can
prove difficult. Unlike bridge, poker is all about
winning. You'll need a good memory, inbuilt risk-
factor judgement, a head for figures and a
seriously spooky poker face.

The objective of this little book is to get you
playing the game as quickly as possible, but
remember: playing poker at the highest level is
the night-work of a lifetime.

GETTING
STARTED

There are many variations of poker, but as we've only got ten minutes, we'll start with Straight Draw poker. This is the simplest form of the game and is played all over the world. The basic rules are quite simple. So, let's get started.

You'll need a full pack of 52 cards and some friends with money. Poker can be played by two people, but between five and eight usually works best.

Each player puts an agreed sum into the middle of the table. This is called the 'ante'. As a beginner, it is better to keep the ante quite low. Before you start you need to establish:

A. The stakes.
B. The finishing time – there's nothing worse than someone suddenly having to leave after winning a huge pot.

First, the cards are cut, and the person who chooses the highest card becomes the dealer. After shuffling the cards, the pack is cut again and the dealer deals clockwise, starting with the player to his left. Each player is given five cards, dealt one at a time, face down.

The object of the game is to make the best hand by an exchange of cards and bet against the other players. The player with the best hand wins. The cards are ranked from the Ace down to the Two.

It is very important to learn the order in which the hands are valued. There's nothing more annoying than someone asking, 'Is a Straight better than a Flush?' (The answer is NO.)

This is how the hands are judged from the highest to the lowest:

1. Royal Flush

A sequence of five cards in the same suit, from the Ace to the Ten.

2. Straight Flush

Any sequence of five cards in the same suit.

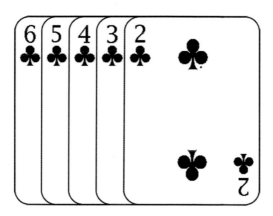

3. Four Of A Kind

Four cards of the same rank.

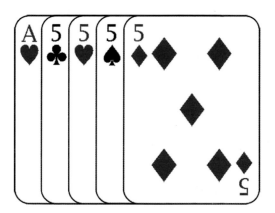

4. Full House

Three cards of the same rank with two other cards of the same rank.

5. Flush

Five cards of the same suit.

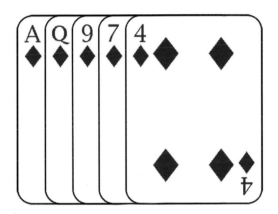

6. Straight

Five cards in sequence of any suit.

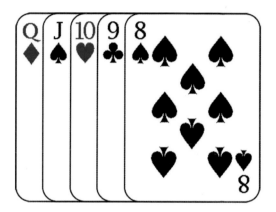

7. Three Of A Kind

Three cards of the same rank.

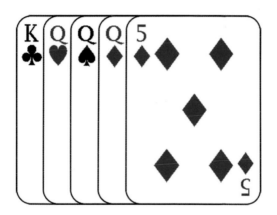

8. Two Pairs

Two cards of the same rank with two cards of another rank.

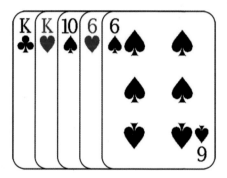

9. One Pair

Two cards of the same rank.

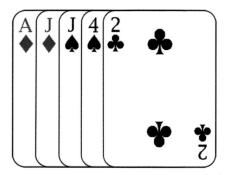

10. Ace High

An Ace with four odd cards.

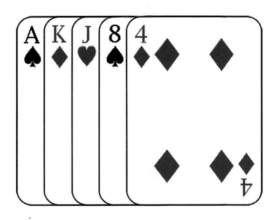

The Highest Possible Hand

The holy grail for all Poker players is a Royal Flush. It is made up of the highest Straight combined with a Flush to give the lucky holder an unbeatable hand.

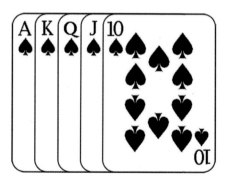

The Lowest Possible Hand

There is nothing positive one can say about this hand. It's just a mix of cards that add up to very little. Even 6, 5, 4, 3, 2 would make a Straight, but the 7, instead of a 6, gives you nothing.

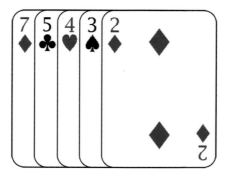

PLAYING THE GAME

Now you can tell a poor hand from a good one, you can start playing the game. Of course, your chances of making a Royal Flush are almost as slim as those of you winning the lottery. But don't worry, a pair of Nines once won the final game of a world series.

Place Your Bets

When all the players have been dealt five cards, they can pick them up and look at them. The player to the left of the dealer has to decide to do one of the following:

A. Fold: discard her hand and take no further part in this round of the game.
B. Check: choose not to bet (this is only allowed if no one has already made a bet).
C. Play: make a bet.

If a player decides to play, he must make a bet and put his chips or money in the middle of the table. The betting then continues around the table. Each player in turn can decide whether to match the bet, raise the bet or fold.

Changing Cards

Once the bets have been matched, the players who are left in the game can discard as many cards as they wish and draw new ones. It is rare for a player to change all of his cards.

The dealer then gives each player new cards. These are given as they are requested, i.e. if a player wants three new cards, they are given together from the top of the deck.

Bet Again

When all the players have their new cards, the second round of betting begins. Once again, it starts with the first remaining player to the dealer's left. He can check, bet or fold. The betting continues until the final bet is called or not. If the bet is called, the remaining players show their cards. The player with the highest hand wins everything that has been staked. This is called the 'pot'.

If the last bet is not called, the player who made the last bet wins the pot. He does not have to show his cards. If the winner has been bluffing, the other players don't want to see it anyway. And if not, they don't really care.

PLAYING
FOR REAL

Sorry, time's up. Your ten minutes are over, and now you have to jump in at the deep end. Find some people with pots of money, sit them around a table and deal the cards.

The important thing is to start playing as soon as possible. Betting, calculating odds, bluffing and assessing your opponents will all be picked up along the way. You'll find tips and tricks on the following pages. If you do get hooked and want to play in the World Series, work your way up in some serious poker schools and buy a thicker book than this one.

Play as much as you can, but be warned: poker is a dangerous game if you find yourself out of your depth. Sadly, the way to learn is by playing with better players. The problem is, better players have a habit of walking off with your money.

As the outrageously wealthy Warren Buffett once said, 'In every poker game there's always a patsy. If you can't work out who's the patsy, it's probably you.'

If you do decide to try your luck at a casino, you'll always meet an interesting mix of characters. And, whatever happens, it'll be a lot of fun. They'll take you as they find you – and your money, if they can.

TEXAS HOLD'EM

Okay, you can now play Straight Draw poker. Next you're going to learn Texas Hold'em. This popular version is often seen on television; it's easy to learn, but a complex game once you've got your cards.

Each player is dealt two cards face down.

Then there is one round of betting. The dealer discards the top card from the pack (this is called the 'burn') before dealing three cards face up into the middle of the table. These cards are called the 'flop' and are shared or 'owned' by all the players.

After the flop there is another round of betting, starting with the player to the dealer's left. He may check, bet or fold. The action continues clockwise. When the betting has finished, the dealer burns the top card from the pack, and one more card is dealt face up next to the flop. This card is called the 'turn'. Then there is another round of betting. When this round is finished, a fifth and final card is dealt. This is called the 'river' and is dealt face up next to the turn.

Community Cards

So, each player has two cards face down and the five shared cards on the table. The remaining players can now make up their hands from the two cards they hold and the five cards that are face up on the table. Now there is a final round of betting, and the betting continues until there is a showdown to decide the winner.

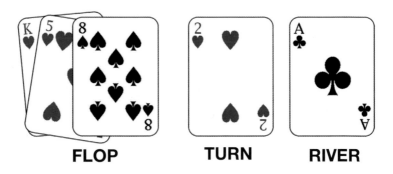

FLOP   **TURN**   **RIVER**

In Texas Hold'em, good hands or equal hands are often produced. Obviously, if the best hand is on the table, every one will 'hold' it. So make sure you've got the cards that will make the difference.

Texas Hold'em is called a 'community game' because the cards in the middle of the table are shared or 'owned' by all the players.

Blinds

Texas Hold'em uses a blind system instead of an ante to get some money into the pot. There is a small blind, which is half the minimum bet, and a big blind that is equal to the minimum bet. The two players to the left of the dealer pay the small and big blinds before the cards are dealt. As the dealer's position moves after each hand, the position of the blinds moves around the table. This ensures that each player must take his or her turn in paying the blinds, so the player to the dealer's left pays the small blind and the other player pays the big blind.

Five-card Stud originated during the American Civil War. In the early 20th century its popularity was eclipsed by Seven-card Stud, which for a long time was the most popular poker variant played throughout much of the United States.

Five-card Stud

In Stud poker some of your cards are dealt face up and some face down. In Five-card Stud only one card is dealt face down, and there is no ante unless agreed by the players. The dealer gives each player one card face down, which is called the 'hole card', then one card face up. Obviously, you can look at your own hole card.

Then there is a round of betting. After the betting, the remaining players are each given three cards face up, with a round of betting between each. If two or more players remain after the last round of betting, they turn up their hole card. The player with the best hand wins.

Each round of betting always begins with the player who holds the best hand of the cards exposed. If two or more players have equal hands, the one sitting to the left of the dealer bets first. Players who fold must turn their exposed cards face downwards.

Two Eights showing. The best you can hope for is that your hole card is another Eight.

Seven-card Stud

Besides getting two extra cards, Seven-card Stud gives you many more chances for getting a better hand. It also gives you more opportunities to bluff. Everyone puts an ante into the pot and then the dealer gives each player two cards face down and one card face up. There is a betting interval, and then the active players are dealt three cards face up and one last card face down. Once again, there is a round of betting after each round of dealing. Finally, you will have seven cards: three cards face down and four cards face up.

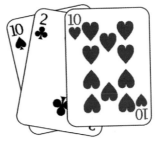

Two Tens showing, but a hand with endless possibilities, even a Royal Flush.

The Showdown

A player shows his hole cards at the showdown and chooses five of his seven cards to represent his hand. The best five cards win the pot.

READING YOUR HAND

This is your hand. At first glance you only have King High, but look a bit harder and you'll see that this hand has a lot of potential. Once you have discarded the Five of Spades, drawing a new card will give you every chance of creating a winning hand.

Let's look at the possibilities:

- An Ace of Hearts will give you a Royal Flush, an unbeatable hand.
- A Nine of Hearts will give you a Straight Flush.
- Any of the nine remaining Hearts will give you a Flush.
- An Ace or a Nine of any suit will give you a Straight.

Any King, Queen, Jack or Ten will give you a decent Pair. Not a great hand, but sometimes enough to scare off players who see you draw only one card.

So, if five players are playing, there will be 27 cards to draw from. There will also be 27 cards that will improve your hand. So your chances should be good. Of course, the other players will probably be holding some of them, but you will be helped by the fact that you will be trying to draw an Outside Straight (four cards that give you a chance to improve on either side), any Ace or Nine. Although you held a King High hand, always analyse your hand carefully before giving up on it.

Now look at this hand:

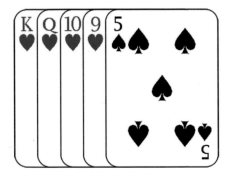

Although it may look similar, it will be much more difficult to improve it enough to give you a chance of taking the money. Once again, you will discard the Five of Spades. But your best chance now will be to draw a Heart, giving you a Flush.

To get a Straight Flush, you will need to draw a Jack of Hearts; this is called 'drawing to an Inside Straight' (because you need an extra card in the middle to make a straight), so the chances will be slim. To draw a Straight, you will need to get one of the four Jacks – easier, but still difficult. Hopefully, you will be able to draw one of the nine remaining Hearts for a Flush. A Flush is not to be sniffed at. It will certainly give you a fighting chance.

So remember, hands that may look alike can provide you with different possibilities. Never give up a chance to draw an Outside Straight Flush, but don't be too optimistic when chasing an Inside Straight.

Flush or Straight?

Do you drop the Five of Clubs to get a Straight or the Seven of Diamonds for a Flush?

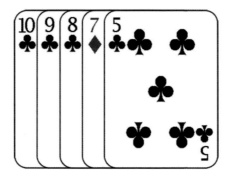

The odds for a Flush are slightly better, because there are nine possible Clubs for a Flush. For a Straight there are only eight possible cards (four Sixes and four Jacks). Remember, too, when making your decision, that a Flush is a 'better' hand than a Straight.

Winning and Losing

Learning to lose is an important part of your poker education. Knowing when to throw in your cards will save you a lot of money. Staying in a game in the hope of getting a vital card is a question of weighing up the mathematical chances. Don't count on luck. Chasing elusive cards is called 'fishing' – and sitting around waiting for a game-changing card can be a depressing and expensive business.

When you've got good cards and reasonable chances of drawing better ones, be bold and bet confidently. Good hands don't come along very often. So when they do, make the most of them.

A Pair of Eyes

After your brain, your eyes and the ability to use them are vital to winning at poker. Good poker players 'see' everything: every discard, pause or trembling hand. They'll notice a player who keeps looking at his cards, a change in tempo when bidding or checking. The body language of everyone at the table. They'll see the possibilities and problems presented by a flop, turn or river. They'll spot the suits and ranks of every upturned card in Stud. 'Seeing' at poker can save and make you money. Of course, the other players will also be watching you. Players often wear different hats depending on their cards, the size of the pot and how much money they're up or down. Your eyes will tell you whether a player is Dr Jekyll or Mr Hyde.

POKER
NIGHTS

Poker nights are a great way to play poker and save money. Hard to believe, but true. All you need is a few friends, a few drinks and some snacks. The idea is that everyone puts in an agreed amount for the evening – let's say £10 or $10 each.

The money is then changed into chips, buttons, matchsticks, whatever. The games continue throughout the evening until the set finishing time. At least everybody will know beforehand the maximum amount they can lose – or win.

Try to think of your poker night as a good night out. How much are you prepared to spend for an evening's entertainment? Win or lose, you should go home happy. You probably won't lose as much as you think and it's unlikely you'll win as much as you hope.

One last piece of advice: be careful who you play with! Try not to play with people called 'Devilfish' or 'Chainsaw', or anyone carrying a gun or wearing dark glasses.

So put on your best poker face, find a game and start playing!

Glossary

ACTION The activity that takes place in the pot.

ANTE An agreed stake before the deal.

BURN Cards discarded before dealing.

CALL To match the last bet.

CHECK A player not betting at that stage, reserving the right to pass, call or raise later if other players bet.

FISHING Staying in a game, hoping to get a particular card.

FLOP The first three 'community cards' in Texas Hold'em.

FLUSH Five cards in the same suit.

FULL HOUSE Three cards of the same rank with two other cards of the same rank.

HOLE CARD In Stud poker, any card dealt face down.

INSIDE STRAIGHT Four cards that need an extra card in the middle to make a straight, i.e. Jack, Ten, Eight, Seven would need a Nine.

OUTSIDE STRAIGHT Four cards that give a chance to improve on either side, i.e. Jack, Ten, Nine, Eight will need a Queen or a Seven.

POT The chips or money at stake in a game.

RAISE Putting more money into the pot than the previous player. The next person to raise is re-raising.

RIVER The last card dealt in Texas Hold'em.

RUNT A hand worth less than a pair.

STEAL To win a hand by bluffing.

TURN The fourth 'community card' dealt in Texas Hold'em.